SIGHTSEEING WITH ALIENS

SIGHTSEEING WITH ALIENS

By Insha Fitzpatrick

Illustrations by Lilla Bölecz

Full Library of Congress Cataloging-in-Publication Data available upon request.

ISBN: 978-1-68369-427-4

Printed in China

Typeset in Black Magic, Freight, Fright Night, and Wolfsbane

Designed by Andie Reid
Illustrations by Lilla Bölecz
Production management by Mandy Sampson

Quirk Books
215 Church Street
Philadelphia, PA 19106
quirkbooks.com

10 9 8 7 6 5 4 3 2 1

To Kayla, my UFO queen

CONTENTS

Introduction

HELLO? IS ANYONE OUT THERE?

Oh, hi! I didn't see you there. Actually, I did, but I was waiting for you to say hello. Now that we've made contact, I have a very important transmission for you. It's a question, actually: Want to go on an adventure? We're traveling to the stars! Here's your space suit, your guidebook, and plenty of snacks for the journey. Sit tight—we're going extraterrestrial!

HANG ON, YOU'RE . . . WHO, EXACTLY?

Allow me to introduce myself. I am your 100 percent human, totally-not-an-alien guide to the mysteries and wonders of the supernatural, paranormal, and extraterrestrial. In this book, we're blasting off to the cosmos! You guessed it—we'll be gathering data on aliens. Together, you and I will rocket through science, discover spacefaring history, meet up with fictional alien friends, and more!

Dig Out the Dictionary!

According to our lexical friend Merriam-Webster, an alien is defined as a being who "[comes] from another world." And what does extraterrestrial mean? Let's break the word down! When you're using *extra* by itself, it means "more" or "bonus." *Extra* as a prefix means "outside," and *terra* means "land" or "Planet Earth." Put them together, and *extraterrestrial* refers to something or someone "originating, existing, or occurring outside the earth or its atmosphere."

WHOA. ALIENS?!

I bet you're wondering, "Wait, are there *really* aliens out there? Can they see me right now? Do they know I'm wearing two different socks?" The best answer I can give you is . . . a big shrug. Who knows? (Also, I wouldn't worry about the socks too much. I'm wearing two different ones, too. That's fashion, baby!)

The topic of aliens is a gigantic question mark. Scientists haven't discovered evidence of life on other planets, but that doesn't mean they're ruling it out altogether. What we know about space and the possibility of life on other planets is constantly changing. In fact, science itself is constantly changing. (Fun fact: scientists are still discovering new chemical elements!) In the meantime, it doesn't hurt to ask ourselves a few questions: What would you do if you met someone from another planet? How do you treat those who are different from you? What do you think the future will look like—for you and for Planet Earth? And is astronaut ice cream actually any good?

How do we find the answers to our questions? We research! We're on a fact-finding mission here and our topic is everything extraterrestrial. In this guide, we'll uncover the stories behind infamous alien sightings, such as the Roswell incident of 1947, and places like Area 51. We'll dig in to what happens if humans make first contact with aliens. And we'll plug in to the world of science fiction and alien movies. Last, but certainly not least, we're going to figure out why exactly aliens are so important—whether they're out there in space or hanging out in the sci-fi section of the library.

So that's our mission brief. Now that you're ready, prepare for takeoff!

Chapter 1

ALIENS 101

"In the deepest sense, the search for extraterrestrial intelligence is a search for ourselves."

—Carl Sagan

Before we can blast off into the far reaches of space, we need to establish our parameters. What is an alien? How do you identify one? What are some common beliefs and legends about aliens? We'll cover all this and more in this chapter. First, let me pour you a cup of gravi-tea. Take a sip of that steaming, otherworldly beverage (okay, it's just hot cocoa), and let's jump in!

HOW TO IDENTIFY AN ALIEN

When you think of aliens, what do you picture? Do you imagine a mob of little green guys, like from *Toy Story*? Or what about a terrifying grey Xenomorph, like from the 1979 movie *Alien*? Or maybe you're imagining a blob of sentient purple slime.

An alien, as we established in our earlier dictionary dive, is an extraterrestrial life form, or as Teresa Shea writes in her book *Investigating UFOs and Aliens*, "a being that originated beyond Earth." So here are the conditions a creature has to meet to be an alien:

- Be alive.
- Don't be from Planet Earth.

Yep, that's it! As you can imagine, aliens don't have one particular look. And sure enough, throughout history there have been countless different depictions—in legends, literature, video games, movies, you name it—of what aliens could look like. But some types of aliens have appeared again and again. Let's talk about a few!

Grey Aliens

The Greys, also known as the Roswell Greys, are often described as being short in stature, with large black eyes, a large head, a small, thin mouth, and long thin arms with four fingers on each hand. They're known for their grey skin or clothing, hence the name. (But why *Roswell*? We'll get into that later.) In pop culture, the Greys

HOW TO IDENTIFY AN ALIEN

have appeared in television series like *Dark Skies* and movies like *The McPherson Tape* (1989). In these depictions, they are shown to abduct and experiment on humans. But in other media, like the cartoon *American Dad*, the aliens are just part of the family.

Nordic Aliens

We've talked about aliens who look really different from humans. Now let's talk about a humanoid (a.k.a. humanlike in appearance) variety of aliens. Nordics, also known as Space Brothers or Pleiadians, are aliens who resemble, well, the stereotypical idea of what people from Scandinavia look like—but taller. (FYI, Scandinavia is a region in Northern Europe that includes Sweden, Norway, and Denmark.) They are described as having blond or white hair, pale skin, and blue (or violet, yellow, orange, or green) eyes. Nordics are said to come from the Pleiades star cluster, which is located in the Taurus constellation. The legends of Nordic aliens were first popularized in 1952, when author George Adamski claimed to have been visited by one.

Reptilian Aliens

Also known as reptoids or lizard people, these are humanoid reptilian beings known for their green scaly skin, clawed hands, and tall stature. Reptilians make an appearance in alien abduction accounts, as well as in science fiction and fantasy stories. Unfortunately, they also feature prominently in conspiracy theories.

Dig Out the Dictionary!

What is a conspiracy theory? Let's check with our pal Merriam-Webster. A conspiracy theory is a "theory that explains an event or set of circumstances as the result of a secret plot by usually powerful conspirators." Sometimes, conspiracy theories are harmless, but often they are based on dangerous and cruel ideas. Conspiracy theories about secret evil groups and world domination are often rooted in racism and antisemitism. Whatever you do, don't buy in to them!

Little Green Men

On August 21, 1955, near the town of Hopkinsville, Kentucky, a farming family claimed to have fought off twelve to fifteen small, unknown figures who appeared at their farmhouse in the middle of the night. According to the August 22, 1955, issue of the *Kentucky New Era* newspaper, they reported to the police that these "little men" had "yellow eyes, long pointy ears, and clawlike hands." Later, the paper would refer to them as "Little Green Men," even though no one had reported the color of the aliens they saw. But when investigators came out to the farmhouse, they didn't find anything to support the story. One theory is that the family may have encountered great horned owls, which would explain the claws and the yellow eyes. Thanks to news reports of this incident, the Little Green Men, also known as the Hopkinsville Goblins, entered the public consciousness.

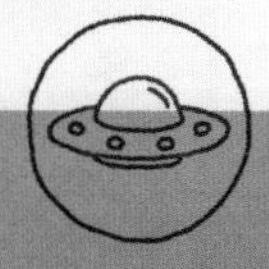

Pop Culture Pop-Up

If you picture little green guys when you imagine aliens, that might be because of the 1995 Pixar movie *Toy Story*, which features three-eyed squeaky toy aliens in a claw machine. These alien toys also appear in future Toy Story movies.

Fairies and Cryptids

Throughout the years, people have speculated about supernatural legends having extraterrestrial origins. The idea is that old tales of fairies from European folklore were actually accounts of alien encounters. Some cryptozoologists (a.k.a. people who search for evidence of cryptids such as the Loch Ness Monster and Bigfoot) have suggested that cryptids may actually be aliens that have been abandoned on Earth. While some cryptid legends have unknown origins, other cryptid legends can be traced back to Indigenous folklore—and not outer space.

Who's That Alien?

Around the twelfth century, in the English village of Woolpit, two children emerged from a pit that had been dug to trap wolves. The children were wearing strange clothes and speaking an unknown language. And strangest of all, their skin was dyed green! One villager brought the two children, a brother and sister, into the village, but the brother soon fell ill and passed away. The girl eventually learned to speak English, and claimed she came from St. Martin's Land, where everything was green and bathed in twilight.

We could go on (and on and on . . .) about all the kinds of aliens that have popped up in folklore and historical reports, not to mention books and TV, but then we'd be here for a light-year. Okay, maybe not literally a light-year, since a light-year measures distance and not time, but you get it. And we have places to go! Stars to see! So let's keep moving. We've got to talk about objects of the unidentified kind.

LOOK UP

What do you see when you look up? Okay, yeah, probably the ceiling. But if you were outside, what would you see? Now close your eyes. Imagine you're in an open field at night. Dried stalks of corn are rustling in the wind. A cow moos in the distance. And suddenly a beam of light shines down, enveloping you. You shield your eyes against the glare and see a round . . . something . . . in the sky, hovering far above you. A hatch opens, and the light starts pulling you up and into a flying saucer. The next thing you know, nine hours have passed and you're back home in bed, like nothing ever happened.

Aliens have been seen all around the world! From Senegal to Iran to Japan, witnesses have reported seeing and even coming into contact with aliens. Some of these accounts have been debunked and proven false, while other accounts . . . well, who knows? The universe is a vast and mysterious place. As ol' Willy Shakes (a.k.a. William Shakespeare) once said in the play *Hamlet*, "There are more things in heaven and earth, Horatio, than are dreamt of in your philosophy."

What's That in the Sky?

While there are certainly plenty of reports of alien sightings, other reports don't involve aliens at all. Instead, they involve their spacecraft. Here's where UFOs come in. *UFO* is short for "unidentified flying object," and it's exactly what it sounds like—a flying object that hasn't been identified as anything we are familiar with. Like aliens, UFOs come in many different shapes and sizes, depending on the report. But the most popular UFO shape is the flying saucer.

"Why a flying saucer?" you might be wondering. "What's next? A flying plate and fork?" Of course, there's a story behind this. On June 14, 1947, a businessman named Kenneth Arnold was flying his plane near Mount Rainer in Washington State. When he looked into the distance, he saw nine mysterious objects that he described as "flying like a saucer skipping on water." (Later, he claimed that he didn't use the word *saucer*. Do you believe him?)

Who's That Alien?

Historical texts describe a craft landing along the Hitachi coast in Japan in 1803. This craft was described as a saucer-shaped boat from which a woman wordlessly emerged, holding a box. The boat from the encounter was named the *Utsuro-bune* (or "hollow boat"). Some claim that the legend of Utsuro-bune counts as one of the first Japanese stories of a UFO sighting, while others deem it a standard Japanese folktale.

The term *flying saucer* gained popularity as the story of Arnold's sighting appeared in newspapers all over the United States and Arnold was interviewed on the radio. So, how did Arnold's story blow up and come to define how we imagine UFOs? To answer that, we need to look at the context of what was happening in the US during this period of history.

In the twentieth century, the media became a central part of daily life. News could spread like wildfire via the newspaper, the radio, and later the television. (And now, in the twenty-first century, we have the internet.) Arnold's encounter was one of the first reported UFO sightings in recent history, and it became widely known thanks to the development of fast and far-reaching reporting. The landscape of how news spread was changing, big time.

After Arnold's sighting and the 1947 Roswell incident (which we'll discuss later), there was a marked uptick in UFO reports. Were people influenced by hearing about UFO sightings in the media? Or was the media just boosting previously unreported extraterrestrial encounters? What do you think? Regardless of the cause, people all over the world have since reported what they believed were mysterious flying objects in the sky. Following are a few examples.

- **Hessdalen, Norway (1930s to present):** Mysterious white, yellow, and red lights have been seen floating in the Hessdalen valley. Some reports have described the lights as moving slowly, while other reports describe them as speeding through the air.
- **Lubbock, Texas (August 25, 1945):** Four college professors claimed to have seen a V-shape in the sky. The spacecraft had twenty to thirty lights around it and seemed to travel at a speedy 900 miles per hour.
- **São Paulo, Brazil (May 9, 1984):** Many people in this city reported seeing bright lights shining from a mysterious object in the sky.
- **New Jersey (July 14, 2001):** In 2001, orange and yellow lights appeared above the Arthur Kill waterway for fifteen minutes. Drivers on the turnpike stopped and stepped out of their cars to see what was in the sky.

According to Science

Some UFO sightings may not be all that unidentified! Identified objects and phenomena that might be mistaken for UFOs include weather balloons (balloons used by scientists and meteorologists to predict changing weather patterns), military aircraft, and weather phenomena such as shooting stars or lenticular clouds. (Look up pictures of lenticular clouds if you get the chance. They're pretty cool looking!)

Visitors from Outer Space

Let's see, what have we covered so far? Types of aliens? Check. Where aliens have been sighted? Check. Now it's about time we talked about the typical signs of an extraterrestrial visit. There are plenty of accounts of alien and UFO sightings out there, but over the decades a few commonalities have emerged as proof that aliens have swung by Planet Earth for a visit. (Whether it's strong enough evidence to actually prove this is up to you to decide.) A few of these common signs include the following.

- **Lights in the sky:** Are they stars? Airplanes? Really, really tall streetlights? Or are they UFOs zipping over the horizon? Strange lights that persist in the sky for hours, days, or even months might be aliens. Or not.
- **Strong scent:** Phew! What's that smell? Another frequently cited sign of an extraterrestrial visitor is the strong odor of

sulfur—a foul, rotten egg-like stink—that they leave behind. Aliens: they fart, too!

- **Crop circles:** Crop circles can come in many shapes, sizes, and designs. They usually appear in fields, particularly corn fields. Over 10,000 crop circles have been reported over the years. Some believe that crop circles are alien transmissions. In 1980, residents in Winchester, England, were stunned to discover a crop of, well, crop circles appearing in their fields. Later, two men named Doug Bower and Dave Chorley admitted to creating the circles, after being inspired by UFO reports.
- **Reports of alien encounters:** If there are eyewitness (or in the case of strong smells, nose-witness) accounts of an alien encounter, it's possible an alien has stopped by! Whether those accounts are reliable or believable is a different story, but when enough of these accounts are going around, perhaps there is something worth looking into.

Pop Culture Pop-Up

The first crop circle story appears in the tale "The Mowing-Devil," published in 1678. The pamphlet tells the story of a farmer who didn't want to pay someone to mow his fields—instead he said he'd prefer that the devil do it! That night, the field was in flames, and the next morning, the field was cut to perfection.

CLOSE ENCOUNTERS WITH THE ALIEN KIND

We've talked a lot about sightings, but what about alien meetings? Has anyone, say, claimed to have high-fived an alien? Or had an hours-long, in-depth conversation with one? People who say they've encountered aliens generally fall into two categories:

- **Contactees:** People who claim to have met, been in contact with, or communicated with aliens are called contactees. Some contactees have said that they communicated telepathically (a.k.a. used their mind to communicate directly with someone else's mind, without speaking or using sign language). During these encounters, aliens are said to bring warnings, messages to pass along, or threats.
- **Abductees:** Abductees are people who have been kidnapped by aliens. They typically report having been abducted when they're alone on the road, but there have also been reports of abductions happening at home, school, or even parties. Why would aliens want to kidnap people? One popular belief is that aliens abduct people in order to experiment on them. Yikes!

Four Signs You May Have Been Abducted by Aliens

Accounts of alien abductions vary widely—happening at different times of day, to different people, in different places. But like with UFO sightings, some commonalities exist among these accounts:

missing time, missing or altered memories, mysterious bruises and illnesses, and the list goes on. Following are four signs you may have been abducted by aliens . . . or just took a really long nap by accident. (No judgment, I love naps!)

1 **You're missing time.** As in, you suddenly realize that hours have passed without you noticing. Maybe you zoned out while watching your favorite anime or fell asleep in math class. We've all been there. But if you feel like that missing chunk of time is a little bit . . . off . . . maybe it's aliens. Or maybe not.

2 **Your memory is a bit hazy . . .** You don't quite remember what you were doing in those missing hours, but you have a strange recollection of . . . something. Maybe it's needles and flashing lights, or lying on an examination table, or the sensation of being on an airplane. You might've gone to the doctor or the dentist. Or maybe . . . aliens?

3 **You're not feeling so great.** Do you have unexplained scars or bruises? Do you feel unexpectedly sick, headachey, or nauseous? First of all, if you're not feeling well in any way, please talk to your parent and see a doctor—I mean it! Don't keep that stuff a secret. Always ask for help and for care. There's usually an explanation for why you're not feeling well—maybe it's a cold, maybe you sleepwalked into a wall, or perhaps you can blame it on the aliens. (But seriously, please see a doctor.)

4 **You're having dreams about aliens and outer space.** This one happens to me all the time! I lie there, sleeping like a baby, and then, boom! I'm traveling among the stars in my dreams. If you're dreaming about aliens a lot, it could mean that you've met one . . . or that you fell asleep watching an alien movie or reading this guidebook. Who knows!

In all likelihood, you haven't been abducted by aliens. (At least, I hope you haven't!) But hypothetically, if alien abductions were happening in your area, these would be the signs to look out for. The galaxy is a weird and wonderful place. You never know what could happen!

Here's the thing: strange and mysterious things happen to people from all walks of life. Maybe something strange and mysterious has happened to you! It's okay to be confused, or sad, or angry, or even excited about something in your life that you don't understand. But as supernaturalists—you've made it through Aliens 101, so you're a supernaturalist now, too!—it's our job to be curious, seek out answers, and, if we need to, get help.

Asking never hurts, whether it's asking questions or asking for someone to listen to you. After all, there's no shame in taking care of yourself and your brain. You want to keep your star system a-okay!

Who's That Alien?

People who believe they've been abducted by aliens might be ignored or shunned for their beliefs—but they're not alone. There are UFO therapists and special conferences specifically to help people who are recovering from an alien abduction experience. No matter what you go through, whether it's an alien abduction or a really bad day, there's always help out there.

Congratulations! That's Aliens 101 downloaded into your database. But we've only just begun our journey. Before we explore some space history, let's build our own rocket!

The Blast-Off Bottle Rocket

With a few supplies and a good dose of science, you can make your own rocket right in your backyard or local park. (Be sure that you have permission to launch your rocket. Don't get in trouble!)

WHAT YOU'LL NEED

A parent or trusted adult to help you out
Paint, cardboard, construction paper, or any crafting supplies you'd like to use to decorate your rocket!
An empty plastic bottle (2 liters or 500 ml)
4 pencils
Duct tape
Goggles
⅓ cup vinegar
1 teaspoon baking soda
½ sheet paper towel
A cork that fits the mouth of the bottle you're using

INSTRUCTIONS

1. First, gather up your crafting supplies and decorate your bottle to make it spaceworthy.

2. Next, secure the 4 pencils to the plastic bottle with duct tape as shown on the next page. Make sure your rocket can stand on the

4 pencils when you flip it over. This will be your launching pad.

3 Now put on your goggles. It's time for science! With your parent or trusted adult on hand, carefully pour the vinegar into the bottle.

4 Next, place the baking soda in the middle of the half sheet of paper towel. Roll the paper towel into a ball with the baking soda inside. Make sure the ball is small enough to fit inside the mouth of the bottle.

5 Now, here's the tricky part! Drop the baking soda ball into the bottle, then immediately plug the mouth of the bottle with the cork. You'll have less than 30 seconds to do this, so move fast! (FYI, when vinegar and baking soda mix, the two react and produce carbon dioxide—giving you an explosive reaction!)

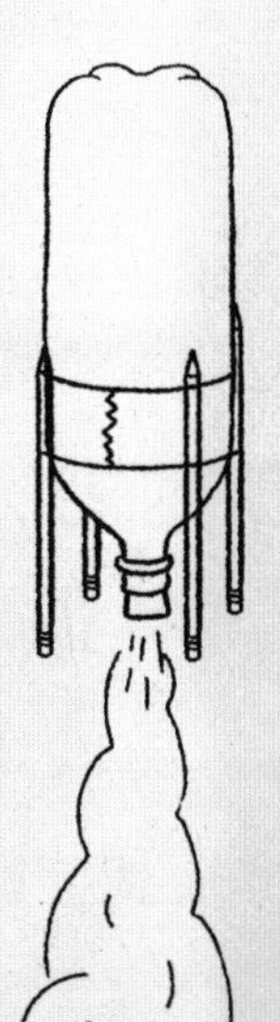

6 Flip over the bottle, get out of the way, and watch your rocket soar through the air!

Chapter 2

RACE YOU TO SPACE

"We revolve around the Sun like any other planet."

—Nicolaus Copernicus

Space . . . the final frontier and possible home to alien life. To truly understand why the possibility of alien life is so important, we need to understand space itself. What's out there? How do we know what we know? And most exciting of all, what *don't* we know about space? My friend, we have a lot of interstellar knowledge and space exploration history to get into!

HELLO, UNIVERSE

The universe has been an ever-expanding mystery for eons. Back in ye olde days of ancient civilization, people believed that we were the center of the universe—literally. They believed that the planets revolved around Earth. Without powerful telescopes and other technology that we have today, scientists of the past had to rely on their powers of observation and deduction to understand space. Can you imagine making sense of the stars and planets with just your senses and math skills?

Astronomy—the study of the stars, planets, and the universe—may date back to prehistoric times. But the very first records of astronomical studies were kept by the Assyro-Babylonians back in 1000 BCE. These records tracked the movements of the sun and the moon.

Why were people from ancient times so interested in things happening in the sky? First of all, just like us, people back then were curious about how the world worked! And secondly, understanding the movement of celestial objects (like the sun, moon, and stars) was helpful when it came to navigation and keeping track of time. For example, sailors relied on the constellations to navigate the seas.

Over centuries, astronomy has developed into a complex natural science that utilizes math, chemistry, and physics. But how did we get here? Let me tell you, it was a long, long journey.

Pop Culture Pop-Up

Ever wonder what the planets in our solar system are named after? Check Roman mythology! Every planet is named for a Roman god or goddess (with the exception of Uranus, which is named after the Greek god of the heavens and the sky). Venus is named after the Roman goddess of love and beauty. And Mars is named after the Roman god of war. But those names aren't universal! Different languages have different names for the planets. For example, in Chinese planets are named after traditional elements, so Venus is the "Metal Star" and Mars is the "Fire Star."

Old-School Astronomy

People in ancient Greece believed in a geocentric world. That means they thought that the planets in outer space revolved around Earth. As you know, that's not the case. Earth orbits around the sun, and it takes 365 days (plus one-fourth of a day) to complete its usual path.

Aristotle, a major Greek philosopher born in 384 BCE, was considered one of the great thinkers of his time and was a huge proponent of the geocentric world theory. Aristotle believed that Earth was the center of the universe and that the stars were fixed in the sky. But why? Aristotle thought that if Earth was moving, we'd also be able to see the stars shift.

Fast forward to Claudius Ptolemy. Born in 100 CE, this Egyptian astronomer and mathematician popularized Aristotle's ideas of a geocentric model—with his own ideas and calculations thrown in. Ptolemy theorized that Earth was at the center of the universe, with the sun, moon, stars, and other planets revolving around it in their own orbits. This theory, dubbed the Ptolemaic system, stuck around until the fifteenth century.

Ye Olde History

The ancient Greeks got one thing right that you might not expect: thanks to their study of the lunar eclipse, they knew that Earth was round. Early civilizations including Mesopotamia and Egypt believed that Earth was flat, with the sky hanging above it. Now, who do you think was the first person to figure out that Earth was round? Here's a hint: it wasn't Christopher Columbus. That's a myth! (Also, Columbus did *not* discover the Americas. After all, the Native Americans and Indigenous people were there long before him.) It was the ancient Greek philosopher Eratosthenes who was the first to calculate the circumference (a word meaning the distance around a circle) of Earth.

The Scientific Revolution

What happened to the Ptolemaic system? The Scientific Revolution happened! This time period marked by scientific discoveries took place from 1543 to 1687 and was kicked off by Nicolaus Copernicus.

Let's set the scene: By the fifteenth century, the church governed pretty much every aspect of life in Europe . . . and that included astronomy! The church adhered to the Ptolemaic system, which meant so did almost everyone else. But there were some who questioned this system. Enter Copernicus, born in Poland on February 19, 1473.

A mathematician and astronomer, Copernicus argued that every twenty-four hours, Earth rotates on its axis, and once every year, Earth revolves around the sun. His ideas were deemed controversial by astronomers of the time, as well as by the church, but he persevered. Before he died in 1543, Copernicus published his findings in a book titled *On the Revolution of the Celestial Spheres*. The church called him a heretic and his book was banned, but his ideas lived on.

Ye Olde History

Other scientific achievements from the Scientific Revolution include the thermometer, invented by Italian astronomer Galileo Galilei, and Sir Isaac Newton's law of universal gravitation.

Born on February 15, 1564, Galileo Galilei grew up to become an astronomer, physicist, and engineer. Galileo was fascinated by Copernicus's heliocentric theory (the theory that the earth revolved around the sun). Through his own research, Galileo figured out that the stars around Jupiter were not stars but actually moons! He also invented his own telescope and was the first to see the stars of the

Milky Way galaxy. In 1632, he published a book which compared the Ptolemaic geocentric system with the Copernican heliocentric system—and concluded that Copernicus was right. The church did *not* like that. Four years later, Galileo was brought before the church authorities and was told to stand down from his beliefs or face death. He pleaded guilty and was placed on house arrest, where he remained until his death in 1642.

COOL, BUT WHAT ABOUT ALIENS?

People in olden times weren't just curious about space. They were curious about life in space, too! (People from ancient history: they're just like us! Except we have microwaveable pizza and TV.)

Let's head back to ancient Greece for a sec. Around 600 BCE, there was a philosopher named Anaximander who speculated about cosmic pluralism, or the belief that there were multiple planets that could potentially have alien life. There were skeptics who didn't buy into cosmic pluralism, such as Plato and Aristotle, but there were believers too. Another philosopher named Epicurus took the theory of cosmic pluralism and expanded on it, speculating that if atoms are infinite, then worlds could be infinite, too.

Later, during the Scientific Revolution, philosopher and poet Giordano Bruno believed that there were infinite universes, and within those universes, there were many planets with life on them. The church, as you might guess, was not a fan of Bruno's ideas or his occult beliefs. In 1592, he was arrested and asked to recant his beliefs. He refused and tragically was burned at the stake.

In the seventeenth century, another philosopher named Christiaan Huygens published the book *Cosmotheoros, or The Celestial Worlds Discover'd, or, Conjectures Concerning the Inhabitants, Plants, and Productions of the Worlds in the Planets*. (Talk about a long title!) In his writings, he speculated about aliens while staying neutral on the subject of whether they existed: "I can't pretend to assert anything as positively true (for how is it possible) but only to advance a probable Guess, the truth of which everyone is at his own liberty to examine." He also attempted to predict what the inhabitants of other planets might be like. He suggested that aliens would have hands and feet and stand upright, but that they wouldn't be humanoid.

See? People have been speculating about alien life since long, long ago. But it wasn't until the nineteenth century that UFO sightings kicked into overdrive.

According to Science

The telescope has a long and storied history. In 1608, a German spectacles maker named Hans Lipperhey applied for a patent for a device called the Kijken, or "looker," that could be adjusted to magnify objects. Then in 1611, Greek theologian and chemist Giovanni Demisiani coined the term *telescope*. (*Tele* means "far" and *scope* comes from the word for "to see.") During his lifetime, astronomer Edwin Hubble (1889–1953) used a 2.5-meter-long telescope to prove that there were galaxies outside of our own Milky Way galaxy. About forty years after Hubble's death, NASA launched the Hubble Space Telescope into Earth's orbit.

Nineteenth-Century Extraterrestrials

One November evening in 1896, residents of Sacramento, California, looked up at the night sky—and what they saw was shocking! Residents reported seeing a strange cigar-shaped ship about 100 to 200 feet long flying above them. And they weren't alone. Between 1896 and 1897, there was a wave of reports about mystery flying ships in the sky—and the American newspapers had a field day. The news printed the stories of witnesses who claimed to see these strange aircrafts, regardless of whether the accounts were reliable or not. These newspapers were the first to suggest that such unidentified flying objects might be otherworldly. People were swept up in alien mania, eventually ushering in a golden age of science fiction. (More on that in a future chapter!) And this was all before astronaut Neil Armstrong even set foot on the moon!

THE SPACE RACE

So how did Neil Armstrong and Buzz Aldrin end up on the moon, anyway? Well, let's crack open the history books and find out!

The Cold War

Between 1947 and 1991, the United States and the Soviet Union were engaged in a tense political rivalry known as the Cold War. Following World War II, the two countries fought over who would have more power and influence on the world stage. But the fighting didn't involve direct warfare as in a traditional conflict. Instead, the Cold War involved strategies such as espionage, propaganda, developing nuclear weapons, and even a US boycott of the 1980 Summer Olympics in Moscow.

Blast Off!

On October 4, 1957, the Soviet Union launched the satellite Sputnik 1, the first satellite sent into orbit around Earth. A month later, they tried to send a dog named Laika into space on Sputnik 2, but sadly, due to the high temperature while the second satellite was in orbit, Laika passed away. The launch of Sputnik 1 in particular prompted the United States to put a rush on their own space programs. Cue the Space Race. Over the next two months, American scientists and engineers worked tirelessly on something they could launch into space, too, and on January 31, 1958, the US sent the satellite Explorer 1 into the atmosphere—and it entered orbit!

Ye Olde History

Buzz Aldrin may not have been the first person to walk on the moon, but he was the first to pee on the moon! Inside his spacesuit was a collection bag for holding urine and, well, when you gotta go, you gotta go. According to historian Teasel Muir-Harmony in her book *Apollo to the Moon: A History in 50 Objects*, Buzz Aldrin's collection bag actually broke and its contents dribbled into his boot while he was walking on the moon. It turns out nature calls even in space!

On July 29, 1958, President Dwight D. Eisenhower signed the National Aeronautics and Space Act, and later that year, the National Aeronautic Space Administration, or NASA, was established. With NASA leading the charge, space exploration took off. Both the United States and the Soviet Union sent male astronauts into space, and in 1963, the Soviet Union sent the first woman, Valentina Tereshkova, into space.

In 1961, President John F. Kennedy vowed that the US would put a man on the moon. Sure enough, on July 16, 1969, Apollo 11, the spaceflight carrying crew members Neil Armstrong, Edwin "Buzz" Aldrin Jr., and Michael Collins, was launched. Four days later, a lunar module ship landed on the moon. Back on Earth, millions of viewers watched Neil Armstrong take his first steps on the moon, followed by Buzz Aldrin. It was one small step for a man and one giant leap for space exploration.

According to Science

The first animals to ever go into space were fruit flies, sent in 1947 by the United States. These fruit flies were followed up by the monkey Albert II in 1949. After Laika, the Soviet Union sent two more dogs, Strelka and Belka, into orbit in 1960, and thankfully, they made it back to Earth alive. Animals such as chimpanzees, fish, frogs, spiders, cockroaches, guinea pigs, and more have been sent into space over the years.

In 1975, the Soviet Union and the United States came to a mutual understanding and ended the Space Race. On July 17 of that year, the US's Apollo shuttle linked up with the Soviet Soyuz shuttle, and two of the crew members, Tom Stafford and Alexei Leonov, shook hands. Even though the Space Race was born of geopolitical tension, it resulted in incredible advancements in space exploration. Not only that, but these forays beyond Earth's atmosphere inspired countless questions about the possibilities of space: If we can travel to the moon, what about other planets? Could humans live on the moon? And is there life out there in the universe?

Ye Olde History

When you think of computers, you might think of a laptop or a desktop gaming setup. But before there were machine computers, there were human computers! Beginning in the nineteenth century, women were hired to perform mathematical equations and calculations by hand. Katherine Johnson, Mary Jackson, and Dorothy Vaughan were three African American women hired to be human computers for the National Advisory Committee for Aeronauts (NACA). The women helped make calculations necessary for supersonic flight and even calculated equations for the missions of Project Mercury (1958–1963) and Apollo 11 (1962). Along the way, they faced sexism and racism but managed to propel major scientific achievements with their mathematical genius.

It's time we get our head out of the history books and hit the road! What do you say to learning about some infamous UFO sightings and hot spots? We'll swing by Roswell, New Mexico, check out Suffolk, England, and even take a peek at the legendary Area 51! Load up on snacks and let's go! Actually, speaking of snacks, I have just the thing for you.

According to Science

So what's the deal with astronaut ice cream? It's essentially ice cream (or something similar to it) that's been dehydrated via freeze-drying so that it doesn't spoil. It's sweet, chalk-like, and brittle. But, plot twist: astronauts don't actually eat astronaut ice cream these days! The International Space Station has freezers now, which means they get the real deal.

Out-of-This-Galaxy Cookies

Looking for some stellar snacks? Here's a recipe for Out-of-This-Galaxy Cookies! This recipe has two phases: First, you'll bake the cookies. Second, you'll create a colorful glaze to give your cookies a galactic look. Make sure you have a trusted adult to help you while making these cookies!

Cookies

INGREDIENTS

2 ¾ cups all-purpose flour
1 teaspoon baking soda
½ teaspoon baking powder
1 cup softened butter
1 ½ cups sugar
1 teaspoon vanilla extract
1 egg

INSTRUCTIONS

1. Preheat the oven to 375° Fahrenheit or 190° Celsius.

2. Add the flour to a medium bowl, then add the baking soda and baking powder, and mix it all together.

3. In a large bowl, combine the softened butter with the sugar and mix until it's smooth. Next, add the vanilla extract and egg. Mix again until smooth.

4. Carefully spoon the dry ingredients from the medium bowl into the large bowl. Mix everything together until a dough forms.

5. Use a spoon or your hands to scoop some dough into a small golf-ball-sized ball! Place the dough ball on a cookie sheet or baking pan. Repeat with the rest of the dough, placing the balls about two inches apart.

6. With the help of a trusted adult, put on oven mitts and bake your cookies in the preheated oven for 8 to 10 minutes. They'll be ready when the edges of the cookies are golden.

7. Put on oven mitts and take out your cookies. While you let your cookies cool, let's make the glaze!

Glaze

INGREDIENTS

2 cups powdered sugar
1 teaspoon vanilla extract
3 tablespoons milk
Gel food coloring (any space-themed color works!)

INSTRUCTIONS

1. Mix the powdered sugar and vanilla extract in a medium bowl.

2. Next, pour in the milk and stir the mixture until it has a liquid-y consistency. Pour some of the glaze into a small bowl. Set aside the remaining white glaze to use later!

3. Now, in the small bowl, add your gel food coloring. You can put more than one color into the bowl.

4. Slowly drag the tip of the toothpick through the food coloring creating galactic swirls. If you want to add more coloring, now is the perfect time.

5. One at a time, gently press one side of the cooled cookies into the galaxy glaze. Place the cookie on a cooling rack with a tray beneath it and let the glaze drip off. Repeat with each of your cookies. Bonus: You can use the remaining white glaze to dab stars onto the cookies with a toothpick.

6. Let the glazed cookies dry for at least 10 minutes, and then it's time to eat! Enjoy your galactic space cookies.

Chapter 3

GET IN, WE'RE GOING SIGHTSEEING

"A towel, it says, is about the most massively useful thing an interstellar hitchhiker can have."

—Douglas Adams, *The Hitchhiker's Guide to the Galaxy*

Whether it's a small, cozy town or a vast, scorching-hot desert, there's no telling where a UFO sighting might happen. Is there a link between all these sightings? Or do aliens just like touring the blue marble we call Planet Earth? Good question. To answer that, let's hop into our own spacecraft and do a survey of alien hot spots, sightings, and abduction cases from around the world.

The Roswell Incident

Let's start with the big one! To this day, the 1947 Roswell incident is still one of the most renowned UFO mysteries.

LOCATION: Roswell, New Mexico, USA

DATE: July 1947

BACKSTORY: A month after Kenneth Arnold's saucer sighting (see page 22), rancher William "Mac" Brazel was making the rounds on his ranch when he noticed a mysterious wreckage in the distance. There was debris—rubber with scraps of tinfoil and wooden rods—scattered everywhere. Brazel reported what he saw to the sheriff, who reported it to the Roswell Army Air Field (RAAF). The RAAF quickly came out and cleaned up the site, taking the debris with them. On July 8, the RAAF issued a statement saying that the object found was a flying disc. But on July 9, they issued another statement saying that the debris had come from a weather balloon.

WHAT REALLY HAPPENED? Believers in extraterrestrial life point to the Roswell incident as proof of a government cover-up. (The conflicting statements issued back-to-back didn't help!) The 1980 book *The Roswell Incident* featured over twenty testimonies from people who claimed to have seen the debris from the Roswell site. One man interviewed for the book, Grady L. Barnett, even said that he had seen four alien bodies in the wreckage of a UFO. In the 1990s, the RAAF released additional statements about the weather balloon, stating that the wreckage found in Roswell was part of Project Mogul, a top-secret surveillance operation to gather information on Russia's bomb testing programs. Today, Roswell has become a popular tourist destination and the subject of television shows, movies, and more books.

The Ariel School Incident

Imagine you're playing with your friends in the schoolyard. You look up at the sky . . . and see a silver disclike spaceship descending! What would you do?

LOCATION: Ruwa, Zimbabwe

DATE: September 16, 1994

BACKSTORY: In Ruwa, Zimbabwe, sixty-two children attending Ariel School, a private school, were playing outside during their morning recess. As the children played, something in the sky caught their attention. According to interviews, a silver disc landed on the top of a hill just out of sight, and the children followed. When the kids arrived, they encountered the inhabitants of the spacecraft, whom the children described as two creatures with large eyes and waxy skin, wearing black clothing. The creatures communicated telepathically, and warned them about the damage being done to the earth.

The children ran back to their school and told their teachers, who were skeptical about their story. But when they children went home, they also told their parents, which led to an investigation. UFO investigator Cynthia Hind and psychiatry professor John E. Mack visited the school to interview the children. Hind asked the children to draw what they had seen, and they created similar drawings: an alien dressed in black and a silver UFO.

WHAT REALLY HAPPENED? Skeptics of the Ariel School incident dismissed the story, chalking it up to a childish prank, a case of mass hysteria, or stress caused by all the media attention on the children. Others believe that Hind and Mack influenced what the children said about their experience. Several of the children involved in the Ariel School incident stand by their story to this day.

According to Science

According to NASA, *astrobiology* is "the study of the origins, evolution, distribution, and future of life in the universe." Astrobiologists study how life can exist—and can even survive and thrive on different planets. Scientists in this field have made some exciting discoveries in the last few decades. For example, they've found new exoplanets outside our solar system.

The Betty and Barney Hill Incident

Also known as the "Hill Abduction" and the "Zeta Reticuli Incident," the account of the abduction of Betty and Barney Hill has shaped popular beliefs about UFO abductions and Grey aliens.

LOCATION: New Hampshire, USA

DATE: September 19, 1961

BACKSTORY: One evening, Betty and Barney Hill, along with their dog Delsey, were headed home from their honeymoon and driving on a deserted highway in New Hampshire. In the distance, Betty saw what looked like a light that was flying upward. The couple kept driving, but the light began to grow bigger and bigger. Barney stopped the car and Betty pulled out binoculars. Barney went to take a closer look at the spacecraft and saw grey beings staring right back at him. Barney ran back to the car and began to drive, but as the couple tried to get away, they lost consciousness. Two hours later, Betty and Barney woke up in their car, with Delsey at their side. Afterward, things seemed off: Betty began having horrifying nightmares, and Barney suffered from an ulcer.

WHAT REALLY HAPPENED? Barney and Betty Hill went to psychiatrist Benjamin Simon, who put them under hypnosis. During their hypnosis sessions, the couple recalled that the aliens abducted them and took samples from their bodies, including toenail clippings and strands of hair. Betty drew a star map that ufologists linked to the Zeta Reticuli star system. Skeptics attributed the experience to false memories and hallucinations resulting from sleep deprivation and stress, but Betty and Barney stuck to their story for the rest of their lives.

The Rendlesham Forest Incident

Considered "Britain's Roswell," the Rendlesham Forest incident is the most infamous UFO sighting in the UK.

LOCATION: Suffolk, England

DATE: December 26–28, 1980

BACKSTORY: At three in the morning, airman John Burroughs was tasked with patrolling the east side of the Royal Air Force (RAF) Woodbridge base. While on duty, Burroughs noticed red and blue lights flickering in the sky. Lieutenant Fred Buran called on several men to go investigate the lights with Burroughs. Upon investigation, the men reported seeing a "glowing object with colored lights" and strange symbols. The lights moved in a flash and disappeared into the sky. Later that morning, the men visited the site and noticed three indentations where they had seen the object. Two days later, the unidentified lights returned, and this time, the men brought equipment with them to investigate. They used a microcassette recorder to record their findings and a Geiger-Mueller counter (a handheld device that detects gamma radiation, or alpha and beta particles). But as they moved toward the lights, the lights once again disappeared.

WHAT REALLY HAPPENED? Some believe that the men may have seen a neighboring lighthouse, but others point to the indentations on the ground and the movement of the lights as proof that it couldn't have been just a lighthouse. A memo about the incident was written by the men for the Ministry of Defense but didn't enter the public eye until three years later.

Who's That Alien?

In 1948, the US Air Force decided to investigate mysterious aerial sightings being reported all over the world. This undertaking eventually became Project Blue Book, which outlined three phases of investigation: one, gather details of the reported incidents; two, conduct an analysis of these incidents and assess the potential threat; and three, contain the spread of UFO information. Finally, in 1974, Project Blue Book was dissolved, but not before a grand total of 12,618 sightings were reported.

The Travis Walton Incident

One evening in Arizona, Travis Walton, a member of a logging crew, went missing for five days and six hours. According to Walton, an alien abduction was to blame.

LOCATION: Snowflake, Arizona, USA

DATE: November 5, 1975

BACKSTORY: Prior to his reported abduction, Travis Walton and the rest of his logging crew were working on cutting down trees in Apache-Sitgreaves National Forest. On November 5, 1975, Walton and his six coworkers piled into a truck. As they were driving, they spotted something in the distance—a strange spacecraft hovering over the tops of the trees. The driver stopped the truck, and Walton hopped out, wanting a closer look. His fellow loggers called him back, but the spaceship shot out a beam of light, and soon Travis and the beam of light were gone. Terrified, the workers left the scene and reported the incident to the police. A search party was sent out to look for Walton, to no avail. Five days and six hours later, Walton's sister received a pay phone call from Walton, who was calling from Heber, Arizona. Walton claimed that he had been abducted by aliens.

WHAT REALLY HAPPENED? Like Barney and Betty Hill's case, Walton's claims have been met with heavy skepticism. Although Walton and his fellow loggers passed polygraph tests intended to verify the truthfulness of their story, polygraph tests are no longer recognized as reliable evidence of people telling the truth. Some speculate that Walton and his crew were in it for a big payday: after the incident, a tabloid paid the group $5,000 for their story. In addition, the crew was facing a big fee for not finishing their logging job, and Walton's disappearance allowed them to avoid paying the fine.

Pop Culture Pop-Up

Walton went on to write about his experience in the book aptly named *The Walton Experience*. This book was later adapted into the terrifying 1993 film *Fire in the Sky*.

Heard of Area 51? This mysterious, super-classified US military base is full of secrets—possibly even of the extraterrestrial kind.

LOCATION: Rachel, Nevada, USA

DATE: Built in 1955

BACKSTORY: In 1954, President Dwight D. Eisenhower approved plans to build and test a secret spy plane known as the U-2. Since this was a top-secret project, the government needed complete privacy. Where do you put secret projects? In a secret base! They chose the Nevada desert and built what is now known as the Nevada Test and Training Range. Over many years, the military tested spy planes and other aircraft. Naturally, everyday people were concerned by what they saw in the sky, wondering if they were seeing UFOs. But for some time, the government refused to even acknowledge the existence of Area 51. Kind of suspicious, don't you think?

WHAT REALLY HAPPENED? Area 51 is a facility inside the Nevada Test and Training Range. Thanks to the secrecy and mystery surrounding this facility, Area 51 has inspired plenty of speculation, rumors, and conspiracy theories. Finally, in 2013, the CIA essentially said, "Yes, Area 51 is real, but it's still top-secret."

Who's That Alien?

Where do alien sightings happen? As we discussed before, alien sightings have been reported all over the world. According to the National UFO Reporting Center, or NUFORC, the top state for UFO reports in the United States is California, with over 15,000 sightings between 2001 and 2015!

Back to our questions from the beginning of the chapter: is there a link among these sightings? While they all might seem pretty different, there is one major commonality among many famous reports of alien encounters: how these accounts reach the public. Like we discussed before, methods of sharing the news—like the newspaper or the radio—helped these reports blow up in a big way.

One interesting aspect of these accounts is how different people reacted to their encounters with the extraterrestrial. If you met an alien, what would you do? In the next chapter, we'll explore the possibility of life in space and what would happen if Planet Earth played host to a few visiting aliens.

Create Your Constellation

Look at the night sky, and you might see a few constellations! Constellations are groups of stars that can be seen from Earth. They are typically named after someone from mythology, like Andromeda (a figure from Greek mythology), or what they look like, such as Leo (the Greek word for lion). The International Astronomical Union (or the IAU) has determined that there are currently eighty-eight constellations in the sky scattered across the Northern and Southern Hemispheres. Throughout history, constellations have been used for navigation, astronomy, astrology, and—my favorite—storytelling! Now it's your turn to tell your own story with the stars: we're going to make our own constellation.

WHAT YOU NEED

A handful of dried beans
Black construction paper
Glow-in-the-dark markers
Scotch tape (or other tape that won't damage walls)

INSTRUCTIONS

1. Take a handful of beans and sprinkle them onto a sheet of black construction paper. This will be the basis of your constellation, so adjust and rearrange your beans however you like.

2. Using your glow-in-the-dark marker, draw a circle around each of the beans.

3. Once you're done drawing circles, move the beans off the paper. Draw lines connecting the circles that are closest to each other, creating groups of connected circles on your paper. Draw as many constellations as you want.

4. Ta-da! Take a step back and admire your constellations. Aren't they awesome? Now imagine you're someone from ancient times looking up at the sky. You're going to want to name those constellations. What do the shapes look like to you? You can name your constellations after anything—your pet, a grilled cheese sandwich, or even yourself. Write the name of your new constellations on the paper.

5. Find a wall and tape up your work of constellation art. Turn off the lights to see your glow-in-the-dark stars!

BONUS: Interested in identifying constellations in real life? There are plenty of apps for identifying constellations in the sky. You can also look up constellations online and see if you can spot any the next time you look up at the night sky. Happy stargazing!

Ye Olde History

The constellations you know in English have their roots in ancient Greek, Roman, and Middle Eastern culture and mythology. But get this: those same constellations have different names across different cultures. Makes sense, right? Take the Big Dipper for example, which is also called Ursa Major. In Chinese, that same constellation is named the "Northern Dipper," and the Ojibwe name for it translates to "Fisher."

Chapter 4

TAKE ME TO YOUR LEADER

"Never limit yourself because of others' limited imagination; never limit others because of your own limited imagination."

—Mae Jemison

We've looked into reports of alien encounters, sightings, and abductions. All of that leads us to the big question: is anyone out there? Right now, we don't have concrete evidence that life exists beyond Earth, but we're learning more and more about outer space every day. Who knows what we'll discover next? Let's explore the possibilities!

FIRST CONTACT

What would you do if someone was visiting your home right this second? Would you be totally chill? Or would you panic and shove all your dirty laundry under your bed? Would you tidy up or make a grocery run for chips? What would you do if you knew aliens were visiting?

If aliens beamed down onto Earth for the very first time, we'd be making "first contact." According to *National Geographic*, first contact is "an initial encounter between cultures that were previously unaware of each other." For our purposes, that means the initial encounter between aliens and humans. Lots of science fiction books center around this exact moment. But what about in real life? Well, there are actually a few secret and not-so-secret government projects to investigate possible extraterrestrial phenomena and prepare us for alien contact. These projects include:

- **The Voyager Golden Records:** In 1977, the spacecrafts Voyager 1 and Voyager 2 were launched into space. On the side of each craft was a twelve-inch gold-plated copper disk. The disk was a record of sounds and images from life on Earth. The contents were selected by a committee headed by astronomer and astrobiologist Carl Sagan. The Voyager Golden Records include a message from former US president Jimmy Carter, greetings in fifty-five languages, various songs and sounds, and 115 images—like the seashore, human anatomy, a family portrait, fallen leaves, and more. These records serve as both a time capsule and a message to any of our extraterrestrial neighbors who might be out there.

- **The Pentagon Project:** Former US Senate leader Harry Reid met with other lawmakers in 2007 to propose the Advanced Aerospace Threat Identification Project, a military operation launched by the Pentagon to investigate unidentified flying objects and unidentified aerial phenomena. The project ran from 2007 to 2012, when it was officially disbanded. Although the Pentagon denied its existence for years, they eventually acknowledged the program in 2020 and announced a new Unidentified Aerial Phenomenon Task Force program.
- **Flying Saucer Working Party:** In October 1950, Sir Henry Tizard, the Chief Scientific Advisor of the UK Ministry of Defense, established the Flying Saucer Working Party. This study was the UK's first official study of UFO sightings and phenomena, started because Tizard believed that reports of UFO sightings were worth looking into. Tizard and four other members investigated three UFO reports, eventually concluding that those cases were hoaxes or explainable phenomena, such as optical illusions and weather patterns.
- **Operaçâo Prato (Operation Saucer):** In 1977, residents of Colares, Brazil, reported flying saucers shooting dangerous light beams. The Brazilian Air Force opened an investigation before closing it four months later.

Dig Out the Dictionary!

Unidentified anomalous phenomena, or UAP, is the most up-to-date term for what we call UFOs. Unlike *UFOs*, this term refers to unidentified phenomena originating from the air, land, and sea—not just flying objects!

The possibility of aliens popping by to say hello is clearly something the government is thinking about. But just how likely is alien life? Can anyone really be alive out there in space? (Other than, you know, human astronauts.) Time to check out the science.

WHO CAN SURVIVE IN SPACE?

First of all, can humans survive in space? Short answer: nope. Long answer: Let's compare Earth to outer space. What allows humans (plus animals and plants and other life) to live on Earth?

- **Air:** The air we breathe is about 78 percent nitrogen and 21 percent oxygen, along with a few other gases. Humans need oxygen to live!
- **Temperature:** Humans can't survive in temperatures that are too hot or too cold. The sweet spot is between 39 and 95 degrees Fahrenheit, or between 4 and 35 degrees Celsius.
- **Radiation:** When you think of radiation, you might think of nuclear power plants, but radiation is just energy moving in particles or waves. It occurs naturally on Earth when organisms break down and decay—and humans are typically exposed to low, harmless levels of terrestrial radiation. But radiation becomes dangerous and even life-threatening at higher levels of exposure.
- **Water and food:** As you know, you need food and water to survive. Food provides nutrients and fuel to the human body, and water does so much: it keeps you from drying up, carries waste out of your body, regulates your temperature, and much, much more. Stay hydrated!

According to Science

Organisms that can adapt to extreme conditions, such as super hot or cold temperatures, are called *extremophiles*. One extremophile is the tardigrade, also known as a water bear or a moss piglet. Tardigrades aren't visible to the human eye—they're so small you need to use a microscope to see them. In 2007, scientists launched tardigrades into space, and the tiny wonders survived radiation and freezing temperatures. Talk about extreme!

So how does space match up?

- **Air:** Outer space is almost a complete vacuum. Sure, air exists on Earth, but in between planets, there's just nothing (or almost nothing) to breathe! But what about on planets like Mars and Venus? Well, Mars doesn't have an atmosphere to breathe, and while Venus does have an atmosphere, it's too hot, dense, and toxic for humans.
- **Temperature:** Technically, there's no real temperature in space. Temperature measures heat, and heat measures the energy of particles. Since space is a vacuum, there are no particles, so there isn't anything to measure! In space, the human body would lose its heat and completely freeze. Planets do have surface temperatures, but those tend to be too cold or too hot for human life.

- **Radiation:** The radiation in space is very harmful and deadly to humans. Even astronauts are not fully protected against space radiation. Lucky for us, we on Earth are protected from space radiation thanks to Earth's magnetic shield, which is called the magnetosphere.
- **Water and food:** Scientists have detected water on the moon, in the form of ice. There's also plenty of water in space as gas and ice. But without living organisms—like the wheat that goes into bread—there is no food.

Space, at the moment, doesn't support human life. In order to survive in space, astronauts live in a spacecraft—such as the International Space Station—that protects them from the cold and radiation of space. On the space station, astronauts eat packaged food that's suitable for eating in space and spend their time working on science experiments, exercising, playing games, and just floating (literally!) through life.

If astronauts want to step off the station, they must wear spacesuits that provide oxygen, regulate their temperature, and protect them from the low pressure and radiation of space. An astronaut's suit has up to sixteen layers and includes a helmet, gloves, and a communication system. Imagine having to put on all that just to go outside!

The oxygen supply is a particularly important part of a spacesuit. Astronauts need it to breathe! If the air supply in their oxygen tank runs out, an astronaut would be in big trouble. Super scary, I know. Life in space sure isn't easy.

According to Science

How long would a human last in space without a spacesuit? Without air to breathe, humans would pass out within fifteen seconds and die. So the answer is: not very long at all!

Wait, What About Alien Life?

According to the European Space Agency, scientists believe that the most likely places that life is possible are on planets similar to Earth: planets with oxygen, water, an atmosphere—you get the picture. We haven't encountered habitable planets like our own quite yet, but who knows what the future and the vastness of space hold?

Look Alive!

If there is indeed life out in space, what would it look like? To know that, we need to nail down our definition of *life*. The characteristics of life in a species include:

- Being made up of cells (or even a single cell!) that allow the body to take in nutrients, produce energy, and maintain the body and its functions

- The ability to maintain a stable and constant environment internally (a.k.a. homeostasis)
- The ability to respond and react to an external environment and its stimuli
- The ability to grow and develop during a life cycle
- The ability to experience metabolism (converting food into energy)
- The ability to reproduce, adapt, and evolve as a species over time

Given those parameters, life can take countless different forms. When you picture extraterrestrial life, you might be imagining a green guy with gills and three eyes, but a microscopic microorganism would also count as extraterrestrial life! Pretty cool, right?

According to Science

How do we get data from space? One way is via the Mars rovers, which travel across the surface of Mars taking pictures, collecting samples, and gathering information. A Mars rover named Sojourner was the first to wander Mars, reaching Mars in July 1997. Since then, NASA has sent four more Mars rovers, and most recently, in 2021, the China National Space Administration sent one named Zhurong.

So, what's next? What's the future of space exploration? We're still far from living on the moon and partying with microscopic aliens, but that doesn't mean space research isn't moving forward.

One exciting development is the Jupiter Icy Moons Explorer, a.k.a. Juice, a spacecraft that was launched in 2023 headed toward Jupiter. Juice will take eight years to get there—talk about a long road trip! And back in 2018, Mission BepiColombo, a collaboration between the European Space Agency and the Japan Aerospace Exploration Agency, deployed two satellites to study Mercury. Those satellites are scheduled to arrive in 2025.

Hey, Planet Earth. How Are You?

Now, scientists aren't just looking to the stars. Scientists are also interested in what lies ahead for Planet Earth. Since we all live on this planet together, what happens to it is of utmost importance. (And if you don't live on Planet Earth—if you're an astronaut or an alien—whoa! Nice to meet you. I'm such a fan!)

One major threat facing our home planet is the climate crisis. Earth's weather patterns and temperature are changing, and not in a good way. Activities like burning fossil fuels and cutting down forests are contributing to the emission of greenhouse gases, or gases that trap heat, and Planet Earth has been heating up.

The United Nations Intergovernmental Panel on Climate Change (IPCC) issued a statement in March 2023 that called for "a major

course correction" to combat global warming. The consequences of climate change include increasingly hot temperatures, dangerous storms, and rising ocean levels. This can impact where people can safely live, whether plants can grow and thrive, and the habitats of different animals. It's bad news for pretty much everyone on Planet Earth, but particularly for vulnerable populations. For example, people living near the coast might face flooding and lose their homes. And right now, pollution from manufacturing plants and oil refineries are causing harm to the people who live near them.

Don't Freak Out. There's Hope!

But it's not all bad news. There are ways that positive change can be made to stop the climate crisis in its tracks—on an individual level, a community level, and on a national or global level.

- **One person can . . .** Reduce, reuse, and recycle! Reduce the amount of waste in your life, reuse what you can, and recycle anything that can be recycled. One specific change you can make is to avoid plastic when possible—plastic doesn't break down naturally and is harmful to the environment.
- **A community can . . .** Plant more trees, hold volunteer trash pickup days, advocate for green energy, and encourage people to take public transportation to reduce carbon emissions. Communities can also work together to speak out against climate change and push their local government to support more environmentally friendly practices, like zero-waste initiatives. We're all in this together!
- **The government can . . .** Invest in public transportation and green energy, regulate major sources of pollution such as megacorporations, and fund scientific research on climate change. On a global level, different governments can sign treaties and mutually agree to cut down on carbon emissions.

Earth is our home, and we're the ones who can make our future a better place to be—not just for ourselves, but also for generations to come . . . and for any possible alien visitors who might want to swing by!

CHOOSE PLANET OVER PROFITS
MY CAT DOES NOT APPROVE!
STAY COOL, EARTH!
TAKE ME TO YOUR LEADER
I HAVE QUESTIONS ABOUT THE CLIMATE
WE ONLY HAVE ONE EARTH
FOSSIL FUELS
YOUR PLANET IS ON FIRE!

The Seven-Day Earthling Challenge

Want to give Planet Earth a helping hand but don't know where to start? Try the Seven-Day Earthling Challenge!

DAY 1: REDUCE, REUSE, RECYCLE

Yes, I'm recycling (get it?) this tip because, well, it's just good advice! The less trash you create, the less you're sending to the landfill. Bring reusable bags to the store so that you can skip the plastic grocery bags, shop secondhand for clothes, and remember to recycle cans and bottles.

DAY 2: COMPOST

Cut down on food waste by composting! It's easy to start your own compost project at home. Just look up instructions online and ask an adult for help.

DAY 3: PLANT SOME PLANTS

Plants help filter pollutants out of the air, and they're just great to have around. Check out your local community garden, grow some plants in your yard, or build a garden indoors. Why not reuse a plastic bottle to create a mini terrarium, or plant some herbs on your windowsill?

DAY 4: MAKE YOUR VOICE HEARD

While we all want to help the environment, a lawmaker can really make things happen. Write a letter (or send an email) to your local government representative asking them to act on the climate crisis.

DAY 5: SAVE YOUR ENERGY

Reduce energy consumption at home by turning off lights when you're not using them, and making sure electronic devices (like phones and laptops) aren't plugged in when they don't need to be. And save your own energy, too—take care of yourself! Get lots of rest and relaxation when you need to. You can't help the earth if you don't care for yourself first!

DAY 6: HEAD OUTSIDE

Need to go somewhere? Consider walking, biking, or taking public transportation with a guardian.

DAY 7: SPREAD THE WORD

Tell your family and your friends about what's happening to Planet Earth. Read up on news about the climate crisis, the environment, and more. Keep learning about what your home world has to offer. Stay curious!

Chapter 5

INTERSTELLAR READS

"Science fiction is the improbable made possible. Fantasy is the impossible made probable."

—Rod Serling, *The Twilight Zone*

To really explore the endless possibilities that outer space has to offer, we've got to look at science fiction. Storytelling—in all its many and varied forms—can do so much: stories entertain us, help us connect with other people, bring ancient history to life, highlight different perspectives, and allow us to imagine new futures. Science fiction in particular has guided us toward the stars and explored what the future has to offer us.

TWENTY THOUSAND LEAGUES OF SCIENCE FICTION

If you've ever wondered what would happen if aliens landed on Earth, well, you're certainly not alone. Time and time again, science fiction has explored this very question about first contact.

But what is science fiction? Science fiction is a genre of fiction that explores stories set in the future, alternate worlds, or outer space—often featuring technological or scientific advances. A lot of science fiction centers around the question of "What if?" For example, what if we lived space? What if the world was taken over by robots? What if the earth entered another Ice Age and giant hamsters roamed the land? What if those giant hamsters could time travel?

Science fiction allows us the opportunity to envision different possibilities when it comes to the future, science, and society. Popular topics in science fiction include time travel, robots and artificial intelligence, space travel, advanced tech, and, of course, aliens. People have been pondering the themes of science fiction since long ago.

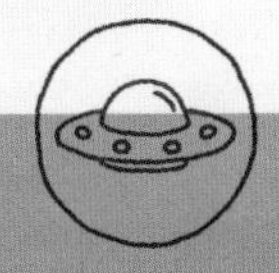

Pop Culture Pop-Up

If you've read the first Field Guide to the Supernatural, *Hanging with Vampires*, you know about Mary Shelley, the author of *Frankenstein, or the Modern Prometheus*. Thanks to her thought-provoking and spine-chilling novel about a scientist who creates a person from body parts stolen from a cemetery (yeah, ew), Shelley is considered the mother of science fiction.

Old-School Sci-Fi

Science fiction dates back to the second century, when Greek writer and satirist Lucian of Samosata published his novel *A True Story.* The book follows Lucian and a crew of men who embark on a long journey. Along the way, they travel to strange and exciting worlds, encounter alien civilizations, and get caught up in a war between moon people, called Moonites, and sun people, called Sunites. What a wild story, right?

For another example of early science fiction, let's crank the time machine dial to the nineteenth century. During the 1860s, French writer Jules Verne's love of adventure led him to publish *Journey to the Center of the Earth* and *Twenty Thousand Leagues Under the Sea*. *Journey to the Center of the Earth* tells the story of a professor, his nephew, and their travel guide as they travel to the center of the earth, encountering prehistoric creatures, an underground river, and a volcano. *Twenty Thousand Leagues Under the Sea* follows another group of explorers searching for a mysterious sea creature. Would you ever travel 20,000 leagues (that's 40,000 miles or 80,000 kilometers!) to explore the center of the earth or investigate the depths of the ocean?

Let's crank the time machine dial again. This time we're headed to the end of the 1800s!

Pop Culture Pop-Up

The 1977 science fiction movie *Close Encounters of the Third Kind* references scientist J. Allen Hynek's definition of close encounters: various types of contact that people may have with extraterrestrial beings. He classifies the first kind as a person viewing a UFO that is 500 feet away. The second kind is when a person sees and feels the the effects of a UFO. And the famous third kind involves a person seeing actual alien beings.

Well, If It Isn't H. G. Wells

Herbert George Wells, also known as H. G. Wells, was born on September 21, 1866, in Bromley, England. If Mary Shelley is considered the mother of science fiction, then H. G. Wells is considered the father of science fiction. What's his claim to fame? During his lifetime, he wrote fifty works of fiction and nonfiction for publications ranging from pulp magazines to medical journals. To learn more about him, let's do the time warp and pay him a visit!

H. G. WELLS: Hello? May I help you?

GUIDE: Hi, Mr. Wells, I am a *huge* fan of yours! Can I get your autograph? Let me dig out my guide—oops, not that one. Vlad the Impaler and Bram Stoker signed that. Oh! And not this one. Not to brag or anything, but it's signed by Shakespeare, or as I like to call him, Willy Shakes—

WELLS: Wait a moment. Who are you? What is this contraption you're holding to my face? And what is *that* contraption over there?

GUIDE: *This* is a microphone. And *that* is the time machine from your book!

WELLS: You built *my* time machine? How on earth is that possible?

GUIDE: It's the power of imagination, my dude. None of this is real. Anyway, enough about me. Let's talk about you . . . It's the year 1897. You've published four novels so far: *The Time Machine*, *The Wonderful Visit*, *The Island of Doctor Moreau*, and my personal favorite, *The Invisi-*

ble Man. What are you working on next, sir?

WELLS: It's a secret. I'm afraid I can't . . .

GUIDE: Please, sir, inquiring minds want to know!

WELLS: Very well. You must not tell anyone. It's a book entitled *The War of the Worlds*.

GUIDE: Go on . . .

WELLS: The book begins with the Martians determining that they must invade Earth to replenish their resources and survive. Soon enough, the narrator, along with other witnesses, sees something strange falling from the sky.

GUIDE: Wait, Martians? Are those aliens?

WELLS: Correct, they are indeed aliens. A long metal cylinder opens up and the aliens from Mars come streaming out. They are grey, with tentacles, and brains that form the bulk of their body.

GUIDE: Cool . . .

WELLS: I wouldn't say these aliens are "cool," considering that they proceed to take over the earth by force using Heat-Rays and their superior technology. The military puts up a fight, but ultimately the Martians win . . . until they're defeated by Earth's microbes, which they have no natural immune defenses against.

GUIDE: Holy wow. That's brutal. So what made you write this story?

WELLS: Firstly, I have a background in science. I used to be a science teacher, in case you didn't know. And I've always been curious about what's out there and about how aliens would evolve in space, where the planets are very different from our own.

GUIDE: Huh, yeah. Like what would someone who could survive on Venus look like?

WELLS: Exactly. I also wished to explore themes of imperialism and invasion. I'm a Brit, after all, and the British Empire covers quite a bit of ground on our Planet Earth at the moment. I wanted to delve into issues of power and ethics and question the morality of colonizing and taking over other lands and peoples.

GUIDE: I think I get it. You sort of flipped the mirror on the British

Empire by showing Martians attacking the British.

WELLS: Exactly. That's what fiction is good for, my friend from another time. Fiction can show us so much by framing it in an entirely different light.

GUIDE: And it's just fun to read! Now I have to run before my trusty time machine zaps back into the present without me—

WELLS: What about your autograph? Who should I make it out to?

GUIDE: Oh my gosh, I almost forgot. Here's my guide. Could you make it out to "an extremely cool, awesome, and amazing supernaturalist"?

WELLS: Hm, very curious. But I can certainly do that. "To an extremely cool . . ."

GUIDE: Wow, you really did it. Thanks so much, dude! I gotta go, space ya later!

Wells and Welles

On October 30, 1938, a terrifying broadcast swept the airwaves as a news reporter witnessed a Martian invasion in New Jersey. The reporter described the destruction and fear left in the wake of this alien incursion. It was horrible! It was frightening! It was . . . a completely fictional radio broadcast narrated and directed by American filmmaker, actor, and screenwriter Orson Welles.

Welles hosted a radio series that performed adaptations of different novels, including *Dracula*, *Oliver Twist*, and *Jane Eyre*. The Halloween episode was an adaptation of H. G. Wells's *The War of the Worlds* and it was a little too realistic. Some listeners, having tuned

in midbroadcast, believed the story was happening in real time and panicked. Listeners called the radio station to ask if the story was true, while others called the police. News of this incident spread across the country like, well, a UFO sighting account!

THE HITCHHIKER'S GUIDE TO SCIENCE FICTION

When aliens appeared in *The War of the Worlds*, they were terrifying threats to humankind. But what about in other works of science fiction? Aliens have been portrayed in widely varying ways over time. These depictions often reflect people's hopes and fears about not only aliens but also the future, the unknown, and even other people who might be different. Ways aliens have been depicted include:

- **Threatening invaders:** *The War of the Worlds* is one example of this! Other examples include *Ender's Game* and *The Body Snatchers*, which portray aliens as threats to humanity.
- **Benevolent beings:** Books like *Dawn* by Octavia Butler feature aliens who want to help Earthlings—a real contrast to the books showing aliens as dangerous and violent.
- **Just like us:** Some science fiction, like *The Hitchhiker's Guide to the Galaxy,* puts a humorous and relatable spin on extraterrestrial life, portraying aliens as not so different from us. They might look different and come from different planets, but they're just as curious and weird as humans.

The Future of Science Fiction

We've discussed science fiction of the past, but how about the genre's present and future? As we've discussed, science fiction help us ask and answer questions facing humanity. Questions we face today might include: What will the future look like? How can we make a better future possible for everyone—humans, plants, and animals? And how do we welcome and connect with people who are different from us?

Authors such as Octavia Butler and Ursula K. Le Guin held up a mirror to our world with their writing. Today, many science fiction authors are doing the same with their work, challenging how we think about space exploration, alien beings, and the future. One such writer is the award-winning Nigerian American author Nnedi Okorafor, who explores topics such as community and racial inequality in her books, like the novella *Binti* and the graphic novel *LaGuardia*. Another author, Mary Robinette Kowal, looks to the past in her novel *The Calculating Stars*, a book set in the 1950s that follows Elma, a human computer who faces prejudice and sexism on her journey to becoming the first female astronaut.

Cosmic Kid Lit

If you're interested in diving into science fiction, there's plenty out there written just for you! Here's a big one: in June 1996, Katherine Applegate and her husband Michael Grant published their first book, *The Invasion*, under the pen name K. A. Applegate. *The Invasion* introduced young readers to the Animorphs books—a series following a group of teens given the ability to shape-shift into different animals. With an alien friend named Aximili-Esgarrouth-Isthill (or Ax for short), the teens take on the Yeerks, a sluglike alien species who want to conquer Earth. Spanning fifty-four books, ten companion books, and a television adaptation, Animorphs explored themes of friendship and family, in addition to heavier themes of death and the ethics of war.

The Animorphs series ended its original run back in May 2001, but the books are still being read today. In fact, decades later, the Animorphs series is now being adapted into a graphic novel format!

But it's not just Animorphs that's getting the graphic novel treatment. Beloved sci-fi media like Star Wars and Star Trek have continued their stories within the pages of comic books, and the cartoon *She-Ra and the Princesses of Power* has a graphic novel spin-off titled *The Legend of the Fire Princess*. It's a great time to be reading graphic novels—there's so much out there to explore!

Just like the writers of sci-fi novels, graphic novel creators are crafting all kinds of cosmically cool stories. Take, for instance, the CatStronauts series by Drew Brockington, which follows an intergalactic team of fluffy furballs as they traverse the galaxy. Or check out *Space Battle Lunchtime: Lights, Camera, Snacktion* by Natalie Riess, in which a baker competes in an intergalactic cooking competition. And if you're looking for something gorgeous and heartfelt, crack open Tillie Walden's graphic novel *On a Sunbeam*, which centers on lost love and found family in space.

Now—and forgive the tangent, but we at Field Guide to the Supernatural HQ love to chat about any and all kinds of graphic novels—if you're interested in graphic novels that take place in an exciting and different world that isn't outer space, you'll want to look up fantasy graphic novels like the 5 Worlds series and *The Deep and Dark Blue*. Happy reading!

Today, science fiction is looking ahead to diverse and richly imagined possibilities and worlds. Between you and me, my to-read pile is a mile high at this point. So what about you? Are you ready to get into some science fiction reading of your own? Or are you already a big sci-fi fan? If so, got any recommendations for me?

Speaking of books, books, and more books, how about we go on a scavenger hunt? Your local library is a treasure trove of extraterrestrial fiction—plus a lot of other cool books. Let's get into it!

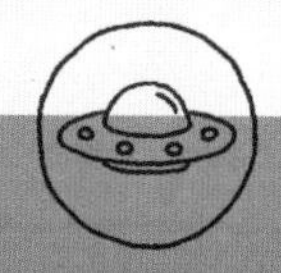

Pop Culture Pop-Up

Want more alien books for readers like you? Check out *Zita the Spacegirl* by Ben Hatke, *Izzy at the End of the World* by K. A. Reynolds, *Crash from Outer Space* by Candace Fleming, *Weird Kid* by Greg van Eekhout, *Sanity and Tallulah* by Molly Brooks, and *Apocalypse Taco* by Nathan Hale. If you're curious about young adult titles, check out *I Hope You Get This Message* by Farah Naz Rishi and *The Kindred* by Alechia Dow.

Library Scavenger Hunt

Are you ready to take your newfound knowledge of science fiction to the next level? Visit your local library and see if you can find these books listed below. If you need help, ask the librarian. (Here at Field Guide to the Supernatural HQ, we're big fans of librarians. They're simply out of this world!)

CAN YOU FIND THESE BOOKS?

1. A book written by H. G. Wells about an alien invasion
2. A series about a kid who lives next door and has an extraterrestrial secret
3. A book about a man hitchhiking through the galaxy
4. A book series written by K. A. Applegate
5. A comic book about a female intergalactic superhero
6. A book about a girl named Nikola who is a scientific genius
7. A Star Wars book written by Justina Ireland
8. A book starring a student named Elara that features terraforming
9. A book written by Bruce Coville about missing homework
10. An awesome nonfiction guide that teaches you all about aliens

ANSWER KEY

1. *The War of the Worlds* by H. G. Wells

2. The Alien Next Door by A. I. Newton

3. *The Hitchhiker's Guide to the Galaxy* by Douglas Adams

4. Animorphs by K. A. Applegate

5. *Captain Marvel, Vol. 1: Higher, Further, Faster, More* by Kelly Sue DeConnick and illustrated by David Lopez

6. *A Problematic Paradox* by Eliot Sappingfield

7. *Star Wars: The High Republic: A Test of Courage* by Justina Ireland

8. *Project Terra: Crash Course* by Landry Q. Walker

9. *Aliens Ate My Homework* by Bruce Coville

10. *Sightseeing with Aliens: A Totally Factual Field Guide to the Supernatural* (the book you're holding right now!)

Now that your bookshelf is packed, how about we move on to your watchlist? Get cozy on your couch, because in Chapter 6 we chat about aliens in television and movies.

Chapter 6

WE WANT TO BELIEVE

"As long as we are engaged in storytelling that moves the culture forward, it doesn't matter what format it is."

—LeVar Burton

From nightmarish invasions to epic space westerns, alien television and cinema have shaped how we view aliens over the decades. And that goes in the other direction, too—our changing perceptions of aliens have been reflected in our media. So what's changed since the heyday of alien encounters in the nineteenth century? Are aliens seen as invading forces or friendly visitors?

ALIENS ON THE BIG SCREEN

What did people think of aliens back in the day? A great place to look is on the big screen. Let's pull up to the superstar drive-in and check out a few extraterrestrial flicks.

Movie Magic

Between the 1930s and 1950s, films like *Things to Come* (1936), *The Day the Earth Stood Still* (1951), and *Forbidden Planet* (1956) told stories about intergalactic travel, alien visitors, and what the future could hold. The movie *Alien* (1979) continued this tradition, focusing on a spacecraft crew that lands on an unknown moon and accidentally brings an unwelcome passenger aboard—a deadly alien menace known as the Xenomorph. The design of the Xenomorph, created by special effects artist H. R. Giger, made waves at the movie theater and changed the game for how aliens were depicted in movies.

Three years after *Alien*, *E. T. the Extra-Terrestrial* (1982) hit the big screen. Directed by Steven Spielberg, this heartwarming movie follows a ten-year-old boy named Elliot as he befriends an alien named E. T. who needs help going back home. Unlike terrifying movies of alien invasions, *E. T.* told a story about finding friendship in unexpected places and embracing someone different from you. It was another game-changing movie that marked a shift in how we think about aliens and impacted generations of watchers. Canadian actor Elliot Page even has a tattoo that says "E.P. PHONE HOME" as an homage to his favorite movie.

Extraterrestrials in Disguise

The aliens featured on the big screen weren't just friends or foe—they were funny, too! The 1997 movie *Men in Black* portrays the top-secret misadventures of two agents belonging to an organization that tracks down aliens and erases the memories of anyone who encounters them. The aliens in *Men in Black* weren't the totally terrifying monsters of *Alien*, and they weren't all friendly aliens in need of a helping hand, like in *E. T.*—they were just plain hilarious.

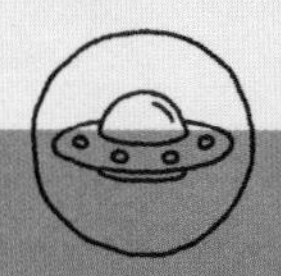

Pop Culture Pop-Up

Special effects artist Carlo Rambaldi, who worked on *Alien,* was also the mastermind behind E. T.'s iconic design. The production costs of the movie totaled around $10.5 million, but 10 percent of that money went toward designing E. T. and other animatronics and puppets in the film. The original and last surviving E. T. animatronic was sold at an auction in 2022 for $2.56 million.

Men in Black, *E. T.*, and *Alien* were just the tip of the asteroid for extraterrestrial cinema. Movies like *Contact* (1997) and *Arrival* (2016) highlight the struggle to communicate with aliens, while movies like *Independence Day* (1996) brought action-packed conflict to movie theaters. When it came out, *Attack the Block* (2011) stood out for its razor-sharp humor, social commentary, and thrilling plot. In the movie, a group of South London teenagers encounter a meteorite and must team up to fight the aliens invading their neighborhood.

Science fiction has always found a passionate fan base in the library and the movie theater, but there's one particular story that put it on the map in the 1970s and '80s.

In a Galaxy Far, Far Away

On May 25, 1977, *Star Wars* came out in theaters. Later given the subtitle *A New Hope*, the movie was the start of a sprawling and epic story that spawned a massive sci-fi franchise. The Star Wars trilogy takes place in a galaxy far, far away, where humans, robots, and aliens coexist. In this galaxy, warriors called the Jedi keep the peace, while warriors known as the Sith strive for chaos and power. Audiences came to root for the brave hero, Luke Skywalker, the quirky Jedi master Yoda, and Princess Leia, the fearless leader of the Rebel Alliance, as they fought back against evil forces. *Star Wars* created an exciting and different kind of world—one where aliens and humans lived alongside each other—with plenty to spark the imaginations of its audience.

ALIENS ON THE SMALL SCREEN

We've discussed aliens on the big screen, but what about aliens in television? There's plenty of fun TV series with an extraterrestrial angle. Take *Doctor Who* (1963–present), a long-running series following an alien Time Lord called the Doctor, who travels through space and time. Another popular series is *The X-Files* (1993–2018), a show that follows FBI special agents Dana Scully and Fox Mulder as they investigate the paranormal, supernatural, and extraterrestrial. (Sounds like they might've liked this guidebook!)

Live Long and Prosper

The voyages of the starship *Enterprise* are known to one and all, but just in case you don't know them, let's get into it: premiering on September 8, 1966, and created by Gene Roddenberry, *Star Trek* chronicles the adventures of the crew of the starship *Enterprise* as they travel through space and encounter different alien cultures. The original show, and the shows that followed, inspired a passionate following.

The original *Star Trek* explored issues of war, class, identity, first contact, pollution, and much more—but that wasn't the only way the show broke boundaries. The cast included Nichelle Nichols, one of the first Black women to star in a major television series. Nichols played Captain Nyota Uhura, a highly intelligent and brave communications officer who specializes in linguistics. When she considered leaving the role, Martin Luther King Jr. told her that she was "reflecting what we are fighting for" and that "for the first time, we are being seen the world over as we should be seen." Nichols ended up staying with the show for many years to come.

During its run, *Star Trek* and its actors continued to boldly go where no one had gone before and inspire fans. The franchise has produced eight television series, thirteen movies, three animated series, games, books, and much more.

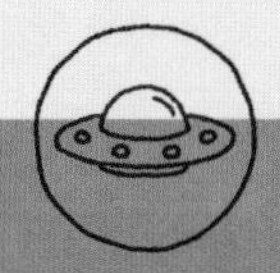

Pop Culture Pop-Up

Many of the stars of Star Trek went on to have long and noteworthy careers. One such actor is LeVar Burton, who played Geordi La Forge on *Star Trek: The Next Generation*. Later on, he would become the host of the PBS program *Reading Rainbow*, a show focused on sharing the joy of reading with kids!

Aliens in Animation

What about cartoon aliens? There's plenty for you to check out: we have Starfire from *Teen Titans* (2003–2006), the She-Ra reboot *She-Ra and the Princesses of Power* (2018–2020), and shows like *Astroboy* and *Sailor Moon*. And if you're looking to have an intergalactic sleepover, a few animated movies you can check out include *The Iron Giant* (1999) and *Metropolis* (2001). Here's a few favorites from the Field Guide to the Supernatural HQ!

- ***Space Jam* (1996):** This wacky, laugh-out-loud movie stars the characters of the Looney Tunes, who end up captured by an alien race named the Nerdlucks. Bugs Bunny and his friends make a deal with the aliens: if they win a game of basketball, they go free. The Nerdlucks recruit talented basketball players to their team, but the Looney Tunes manage to recruit none other than basketball legend Michael Jordan.

- ***Lilo and Stitch* (2002):** In this Disney movie, an alien named Experiment 626 escapes and lands in Hawaii. A girl named Lilo Pelekai and her older sister, Nani, take in Experiment 626 as their new pet dog and name him Stitch. Along the way, Stitch and Lilo learn about the meaning of family.
- ***Steven Universe*:** Airing from 2013 to 2019, this funny and heartfelt cartoon follows a boy named Steven who is raised by three aliens named Pearl, Amethyst, and Garnet. As Steven grows up, he must face questions of the past, who he is, and his own alien powers, all while embracing the power of love.

Pop Culture Pop-Up

In addition to being a beloved cartoon show, *Steven Universe* is also an award-winning one! The show has won accolades for its voice acting, animation, storytelling, and LGBTQ representation. In 2019, *Steven Universe* won both a GLAAD Media Award and a Peabody Award.

ALIENS OF THE SUPERHERO KIND

Here's a type of alien we haven't talked about much: the superhero kind! Sometimes, superheroes are regular humans, like Batman and Captain America. But dig into superhero lore, and you'll find that some superheroes are actually aliens, like Superman. Yep, Superman is an alien. Kal-El, or Clark Kent, is a Kryptonian alien sent to Earth as a baby and adopted by two farmers. When Superman discovers his superpowers, he uses them for good, fighting to protect the city of Metropolis. Created by writer Jerry Seigel and artist Joe Shuster, Superman as we know him first appeared in *Action Comics* #1 on April 18, 1938. In addition to being fun and thrilling adventures, the Superman comics tackled important issues that everyday people face: discrimination and environmental justice, among other issues.

From E. T. and the Xenomoprhs to Stitch and Superman, how aliens have been portrayed—and our relationship to them—has changed a lot over the years. Aliens might have started as scary threats, but now we have stories about aliens who are heroic, kind, and not so different from us.

To My Future Self

When I was a kid, I wrote a time capsule letter to myself. A time capsule is a container in which you place notes, pictures, news articles, and anything else that you want your future self to see. My time capsule letter was really important to me, and you can try writing one yourself!

For a time capsule, you'll need a sturdy container that you can close or seal up. I used an old shoebox. Here are some things you can put in your capsule:

- Your own sketches or paintings
- Photos of your family, your pet, or your friends
- Special keepsakes you'd like your future self to have
- Newspaper or magazine clippings
- A list of your favorite TV shows, movies, songs, games, and books
- A note from someone you love, like a family member or a friend
- Last but certainly not least, a letter to yourself. You can talk about how you feel right now, or your hopes and dreams for the future, or anything else you feel like writing!

In addition to a letter to yourself, I have a bonus letter for you to write if you're up for it: a letter addressed to aliens! Just think—if you were pen pals with an alien, what would you say? What about

Planet Earth and humanity would you want to share? Here's my suggestion for what to include:

- Start off with a greeting like "Hi, my name is . . ." Introduce yourself! Who are you?
- Talk about your life on Earth! What's it like to be you?
- What does an alien need to know about humans? Do you think aliens would like living on Earth? How can aliens get along with humans?
- Are there any fun facts about Earth and its inhabitants that you want aliens to know? Maybe you can tell them about the ocean, or vampire bats, or *Titan arum*, the corpse flower. Earth is an exciting place, after all!
- Finally, what questions do you have for aliens? For example: What's their home planet like? What language do they speak? What did they eat for dinner today?

When you're done, stick your letters into your time capsule, and seal it up. Choose a date in the future to open it: a year from now, five years, or even ten years—whatever you like! What do you think the world will be like when you open your time capsule. What about you yourself?

DATE: 2024
TITLE: SIGHTSEEING WITH ALIENS
SIGHTSEEING WITH ALIENS
THE HITCHHIKER'S GUIDE to EARTH
ST★R
★RS

Conclusion

WELCOME TO EARTH!

"There's nothing new under the sun, but there are new suns."

—Octavia Butler

Hey there—nice to meet you! I know what you're thinking: "What are you talking about? I've already met you, extremely cool guide person." That may be true, but look at us! Look at how far we've come. Who would have thought we'd traverse the galaxy together?

We've traveled the interstellar superhighway together to find spots where aliens and UFOs may have landed. We speculated about the possibility of life in outer space. We dug into history, science, literature, and pop culture of the extraterrestrial kind. And best of all, we talked about how to create a better future for Planet Earth, for ourselves, and for any alien visitors who might beam down. It's been the best space adventure. What more could a supernaturalist ask for?

Actually, I do have one last question for you: what would you do if you met an alien? I hope, after all that you studied and learned and questioned, that you'd face the unknown—whether that's an alien showing up on your doorstep, a new kid at your school, or even the big question mark of the future—with an open mind and open arms.

After all, the best way to face the unknown is to get to know it. There is so much to learn about the world out there, and that's pretty amazing. Stay curious, and you'll be surprised at where you'll end up.

WAIT, BUT *IS* ANYONE OUT THERE?

So to answer our first question of this guide, is anyone out there? Maybe. Who knows what or who is out there? One thing I do know is that we aren't alone on this planet we call Earth. The universe is full of possibilities. If you want to find out more, you can—pack your guide, and get out there!

BIBLIOGRAPHY

Incoming transmission! Read on for the sources consulted in the writing of this guide to everything extraterrestrial.

Arora, Akash. "What Martin Luther King Jr. Taught Star Trek Actor Nichelle Nichols About Representation." *SBS*, August 1, 2022. https://www.sbs.com.au/news/article/what-martin-luther-king-taught-star-trek-actor-nichelle-nichols-about-representation/8wntuxr9r. Accessed September 12, 2023.

Boardman, Adam Allsuch. *An Illustrated History of UFOs*. London: Nobrow, 2020.

"Career Path Suggestions: Astrobiology." *NASA*, August 30, 2022. https://astrobiology.nasa.gov/career-path-suggestions. Accessed September 12, 2023.

Fox, Erin. "5 Incredible Breakthroughs in Astrobiology (and Why They Matter)." *Florida Tech News*, October 24, 2016. https://news.fit.edu/academics-research/5-incredible-breakthroughs-astrobiology. Accessed September 12, 2023.

Halls, Kelly Milner. *Alien Investigation: Searching for the Truth about UFOs and Aliens*. Minneapolis, MN: Millbrook Press, 2012.

Holloway, April. "The Green Children of Woolpit: Legendary Visitors from Another World." *Ancient Origins*, updated January 20, 2022. https://www.ancient-origins.net/myths-legends-europe/green-children-of-woolpit-002347. Accessed September 12, 2023.

"World's Top Climate Scientists Issue 'Survival Guide for Humanity,' Call for Major Course Correction." CNBC, March 20, 2023. https://www.cnbc.com/2023/03/20/ipcc-report-on-climate-un-scientists-call-for-course-correction.html. Accessed September 12, 2023.

Janssen, Volker. "How the 'Little Green Men' Phenomenon Began on a Kentucky Farm." History.com, January 2, 2020. https://www.history.com/news/little-green-men-origins-aliens-hopkinsville-kelly. Accessed September 12, 2023.

Kentucky New Era. "Story of Space-Ship, 12 Little Men Probed Today." August 22, 1955. Accessed September 12, 2023, via Google News. https://news.google.com/newspapers?id=HeYrAAAAIBAJ&pg=2838,3341366.

Kettelkamp, Larry. *ETs and UFOs: Are They Real?* New York: Morror Junior Books, 1996.

Landau, Elaine. *UFOs*. Brookfield, CT: Millbrook Press, 1996.

Marcovitz, Hal. *UFOs and Alien Encounters: Are They Real?* San Diego, CA: ReferencePoint Press, 2022.

Mason, Paul. *Investigating UFOs and Aliens*. Mankato, MN: Capstone Press, 2009.

McCollum, Sean. *Handbook to UFOs, Crop Circles, and Alien Encounters*. Mankato, MN: Capstone, 2016.

Morancy, Joalda, and Amy Grimes. *Aliens: Join the Scientists Searching Space for Extraterrestrial Life*. New York: Neon Squid, 2022.

Owoseje, Toyin. "Original Animatronic 'E.T.' Model Used in Spielberg Classic Sells for $2.56 Million." CNN, December 19, 2022. https://www.cnn.com/style/article/et-model-auction-intl-scli/index.html. Accessed September 12, 2023.

Pipe, Jim. *Aliens*. New York: Gareth Stevens Publishing, 2013.

"Project Blue Book." History.com, February 22, 2010. https://www.history.com/topics/paranormal/project-blue-book. Accessed September 12, 2023.

Shea, Therese. *Investigating UFOs and Aliens*. New York: Britannica Educational Publishing, 2014.

Spignesi, Stephen, and William J. Birnes. *The Big Book of UFO Facts, Figures & Truth: A Comprehensive Examination*. New York: Skyhorse Publishing, 2019.

Tieck, Sarah. *Aliens*. Minneapolis, MN: ABDO Publishing Company, 2015.

Walker, Kathryn. *Mysteries of Alien Visitors and Abductions*. New York: Crabtree Publishing Company, 2008.

———. *Mysteries of UFOs*. New York: Crabtree Publishing Company, 2008.

Wilson, Colin. *UFOs and Aliens*. 1st American ed. New York: DK Publishing, 1997.